Messi

The Complete Story of a Football Superstar

100+ Interesting Trivia Questions, Interactive Activities, and Random, Shocking Fun Facts Every "La Pulga" Fan Needs to Know

HOUSE OF BALLERS

YOUR FREE BONUS!

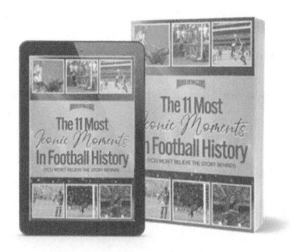

>> SCAN THE QR CODE BELOW TO GAIN EXCLUSIVE ACCESS <<

Contents

INTRODUCTION

From a very tender age, it always seemed clear that Lionel Andres Messi was going to be a special player. But not even his grandmother, who is credited with being the first to spot his precocious talent, had no inkling that she was watching arguably the finest player to ever play football.

By the time he was 16 though, there were no longer any doubts as to what the young Argentine represented – Diego Maradona's true heir. Right now, for most people, he has not only matched Maradona's legacy, but he has also surpassed it by several country miles. And he is not done yet.

Blessed with insane close control, unstoppable explosive power, incredible turning radius, and unparalleled ball striking, Lionel Messi has left his footprints on the sands of time, and they are huge. But perhaps his greatest weapon is a wand of a left foot, the sweetest ever given to a football player. Capable of mazy runs that take out multiple opponents; able to provide great creativity and vision, and possessing the finishing ability to match, Lionel Messi has come, seen, and conquered all before him.

With his tournament-winning displays at the 2022 World Cup, Lionel Messi finally completed football and put to bed any arguments about his status in the history of football. Not that it was ever really in doubt.

The iconic moments are too numerous to cover. From the famous "Ankara Messi, Ankara Messi" chant as he raced through multiple challenges to slam home a fitting finish; to his Maradona-esque mazy run through six opponents, Lionel Messi has left more people on the edge of their seats than anybody in history.

Respected by his teammates, revered by his fans, and feared by his opponents, Messi has found an answer to all questions ever asked of him.

"He doesn't score against English clubs?"

No problem! Two UCL final-winning displays and a four-goal salvo against Arsenal later and there was no longer a question.

"He doesn't score headers"

A glorious header later to win the UCL against Manchester United and there was no longer a question.

"No international trophy"

And he delivered the Copa America and 2022 World Cup to seal his status as the greatest pair of feet to play the game.

His career has been filled with examples of him defeating the odds single handedly and this book is your guide to the most intriguing and exciting moments of his career.

If you'd like to have the glorious facts and statistics behind his career in your palms, then this trivia book is surely for you. We have compiled the best trivia questions and stories from the career of *La Atomica Pulga* (The Atomic Flea) for you in this book.

Unstoppable, irrepressible, and incredible, this is the story of Lionel Messi, the diminutive young footballer that arguably outgrew every footballer of his generation and more!

Sit back and relax!

BIRTH & CHILDHOOD

"I have seen the player who will inherit my place in Argentine soccer and his name is Messi. Messi is a genius."

- Diego Maradona

Lionel Andres Messi was born on 24 June 1987 in Rosario, Santa Fe, as the third child of Celia Maria Cuccittini and Jorge Horacio Messi. His father, Jorge, worked as a steel factory manager, while his mother, Celia, worked in a magnetic oil manufacturing workshop and occasionally as a cleaner. Messi has two elder brothers, Rodrigo and Matias, and a younger sister, Maria Sol. Messi's paternal grandparents were of Spanish and Italian descent, immigrants from the northcentral Adriatic-Marche region of Italy. His maternal grandparents however, were of pure Italian descent.

Messi was brought up in Rosario, the largest city in the central Argentinian province of Santa Fe, and spent most of his childhood in the company of his siblings. By the time Messi reached 10 years of age, he was noticeably smaller than boys his age, and was later diagnosed with Growth Hormone Deficiency (GHD), a condition that severely affected his physical development and seriously threatened his future career.

At 11 years old, he was only 130 cm tall, the average height for 8-year-old kids. The origin of his growth problem was attributed to hypophysis, a defect in the pituitary gland which controls the release of hormones associated with growth and development. Tests were conducted to determine if Messi needed specialist care to restore normal growth and development of his bones and muscles.

Messi's parents sought specialist treatment for their son and a cure was found, although it proved so expensive that the family could not foot the entire bill before the completion of the treatment, as his father's insurance plan could only cover two years of the regimen of nightly growth hormone injections that cost about a thousand dollars monthly.

10 Trivia Questions

1. How many siblings does Lionel Messi have?

   A. 2

   B. 3

   C. 4

   D. 5

2. In which Argentine city was Messi born?

   A. Buenos Aires

   B. Cordoba

   C. Rosario

   D. La Plata

3. In which of these months was Messi born?

   A. April

   B. May

   C. June

   D. July

4. Which family member discovered Messi's talent?

   A. Father

   B. Mother

   C. Sister

   D. Grandmother

5. Messi was born in the year_____?

    A. 1987

    B. 1988

    C. 1989

    D. 1990

6. In his childhood, Messi was diagnosed with _____?

    A. Cancer

    B. Hormone disorder

    C. Heart disease

    D. Lung disease

7. What is Lionel Messi's middle name?

    A. Alvaro

    B. Antonio

    C. Andres

    D. Andrade

8. What is the name of Messi's sister?

    A. Elise

    B. Margret

    C. Monica

    D. Maria Sol

9. Messi's father was a manager in a _____?

    A. Bakery

    B. Steel factory

    C. Tannery

    D. Armory

10. What was the estimated monthly cost of Messi's treatment?

    A.   100 dollars

    B.   1,000 dollars

    C.   10,000 dollars

    D.   10 dollars

10 Trivia Answers

1. B – 3

2. C – Rosario

3. C – June

4. D – Grandmother

5. A – 1987

6. B – Hormone disorder

7. C – Andres

8. D – Maria Sol

9. B – Steel factory

10. B – 1,000 dollars

WORD SEARCH #1

```
M J M E E P W J C Y Z R O X Z N Z L A T
O T Z O P W R M T Y E L F Y E V M B N Q
I X M F Q A R W N Q L A G I L L L P I Y
V N U W H N O C R D K P X T A M T L T Y
W Q O G J C S Y O S B U G G G K N T N T
J G Z Y G U A B D K J L B G C C N E E R
V J O U X I R O N T O G C U B G W S G W
E A Q F T M I R O C P A E X H V V L R P
O B O L B Z O Y L W A R G K E Z E Z A O
D M I K Y C W Y L Y I R L F S N L G Z X
T M G Z Y S L R A W F D P N O N B A N D
P A K Z T L X N B S D Q C I J N L T D P
K J R S L S A L B R N S L Z G O K L G E
I P S A A H L V Z N W C J H G J L Z A D
D M K U N K P P J H Y E N M S F V F F E
L O E D E Y V T F E J R J E G Z F H H W
J X A S P C P U C D L R O W R Z M R L B
D W L N S C D H N L A F P B F K G R Y U
X O G E K I X Z V I D I X D L E I E A M
D H B Z O L U H B G I S P W A B S T X U
```

1. Golazo
2. Argentina
3. Ballon D' Or
4. World Cup
5. Lionel

6. Messi
7. La Pulga
8. Leo
9. Penalty
10. Rosario

FORAY INTO FOOTBALL AND YOUTH CAREER

"In my entire life, I have never seen a player of such quality and personality at such a young age... Before a game, you can plan for everything. But Messi can produce a move that no one expects and change the game in an instant."

- Fabio Capello

Growing up in a tight-knit football-loving household, Lionel Messi was passionate about the round leather game from a very young age. His grandmother, Celia-Oliveira's intuitiveness led her to believe he could become a really good footballer when he was only four years old. His brothers, Matias and Rodrigo, taught him how to kick a ball, and he soon began playing with them and his cousins, Emanuel and Maximiliano Biancucchi, both of whom later became professional footballers as well.

Celia-Oliveira was very enthusiastic about Messi's prospects of becoming a footballer that she personally took him to his first training session at Grandoli, a local football club he joined as a five-year old. She also persuaded his parents to buy him a pair of football boots, and also tasked the then coach at Grandoli, Salvador Aparicio, to include little Lionel in his matchday squad. Aparicio was impressed by Messi's talents and vowed to take him to a bigger academy.

Messi joined the youth ranks of Rosario-based club Newell's Old Boys in 1994, and scored close to 500 goals during his six-year stay at the club. He was part of the renowned "Machine of 87," a group of superbly talented and almost unbeatable Newell's youth side who got their nickname from their year of birth – 1987. The group of boys often entertained fans, and performed ball tricks during the half-time interval of their first team's home matches.

When Messi's growth hormone problem surfaced, his club at the time, Newell's Old Boys, agreed to contribute financially towards his treatment, but ultimately never came through. He had a trial at Buenos Aires with River Plate, whose playmaker, Pablo Aimar he idolized, but they also refused to put forward funds for his recruitment and medical expenses.

It was his paternal grandparents, Eusebio Mess and Rosa Maria Perez, who lived at Catalonia that found help by convincing a member of Barcelona's management to enroll Messi into their youth side and cover the remaining costs of his treatment.

Though at the time it was not permissible for European clubs to sign foreign players of Messi's age, then Barcelona director, Charly Rexach, pushed for Messi's signature, despite stiff resistance from the club's board. Newell's had given Barcelona an ultimatum in November 2000 to show commitment towards Messi's signature or risk losing him to another club. This prompted Rexach to hurriedly sign Messi's first contract on a paper napkin.

Messi's family moved with him to Barcelona in February 2001, staying in an apartment near the club's Camp Nou stadium. Messi did not play much football in his first year at Barcelona's La Masia academy due to a dispute between Newell's and his new club.

He kept mostly to himself at the academy, leading to speculation amongst his teammates as to whether he was dumb. He also felt homesick as his mother and siblings returned to Rosario, leaving him with his father and some distant relatives. From February 2002, Barcelona were allowed to play Messi in all competitions, and he soon became friends with some of his teammates, most notable of whom were Gerard Pique and Cesc Fabregas.

Messi became an integral part of Barcelona's Baby Dream Team, touted by some as the club's greatest-ever youth side. He scored 36 goals in 30 appearances for *Cadetes* A in his first full season, helping them win an unprecedented treble of league and both Catalan and Spanish cups.

The 4-1 victory over derby rivals, Espanyol, is known in club legend as the *Partido de la Mascara* (the final of the mask). Messi was only allowed to start the game if he wore a plastic face protector due to a cheekbone injury. The mask hindered him, so he took it off and scored a brace in ten minutes before he was brought off.

Messi received an offer, along with Fabregas to join Arsenal, but he declined. Fabregas accepted the offer and moved to Arsenal, with Pique joining Manchester United soon after. Messi went on to make 97 youth appearances for Barcelona across under-13, under-16, under-19 and reserve team levels, scoring 89 times. In the 2003/04 season, he debuted for a club record 5 youth teams and scored 5 goals in 15 appearances for the now defunct Barcelona C. In the 2004/05 season, he scored 6 goals in 17 appearances for Barcelona B (reserves) before he was promoted to the senior team during the course of that season.

10 Trivia Questions

1. Where did Messi start to play football?

    A. Grandoli

    B. Newell's Old Boys

    C. River Plate

    D. Barcelona

2. At what age did Messi join Newell's Old Boys?

    A. 7

    B. 6

    C. 5

    D. 4

3. Messi joined Barcelona's youth academy in the year _____?

    A. 2003

    B. 2002

    C. 2001

    D. 2000

4. Which club made an offer to Messi in 2003?

    A. Arsenal

    B. Real Madrid

    C. Juventus

    D. Inter Milan

5. When did Messi become eligible to play in all competitions for Barcelona's youth team?

    A. 2000

    B. 2001

    C. 2002

    D. 2003

6. How many goals were scored by Messi in the *Partido de la mascara?*

    A. 0

    B. 3

    C. 2

    D. 5

7. In which season did Messi score the most goals in his youth career at Barcelona?

    A. 2000/01

    B. 2001/02

    C. 2002/03

    D. 2003/04

8. How many trophies did Messi win with Barcelona's Baby Dream Team in 2002/03?

    A. 0

    B. 1

    C. 5

    D. 3

9. At which club was Messi a part of the Machine of 87?

    A. River Plate

    B. Newell's Old Boys

    C. Grandoli

    D. Barcelona

10. How many games did Messi play in the 2002/03 season for Barcelona's *Cadetes A*?

    A. 30

    B. 32

    C. 34

    D. 36

10 Trivia Answers

1. A – Grandoli

2. B – 6

3. D – 2000

4. A – Arsenal

5. C – 2002

6. C – 2

7. C – 2002/03

8. D – 3

9. B – Newell's Old Boys

10. A – 30

WORD SEARCH #2

```
L Y Y R G C H A M P I O N S L E A G U E
Y R R M M A O U K B S M W H R P D J H A
E R E B O U W S U S R V E O E D B V P H
R K K X P Q G E K W A N L Y L H D J D Y
T A A E K X P U G W D O A E B X E I V L
Z W M S W C P A V K K A L R B R H L N M
A Q Y K A R F J B Q R S I L I N R G G N
F B A H H Q R G V D Z I G E R A N P B C
Z L L Q C W E N Y U T U A D D M Q G A L
W M P E D D K M M F D F V A T V G B R I
F V M N S H I X P J S P C P K I M U C A
A J H M E W R J C P T I H O K G D S E R
T K P Q D S T T O P R P T C L X C W L Q
K V T L Z O S E I E M K Y Y C A N I O G
Z X Q X X E W H M Q S X P A C Y E N N X
Q A L J H S F A G G E T M U U O C G A M
L P S G Z L A Z S G Z P L U G Q P G N F
K B J N X P X S E L N R R Z D N V D V I
Q M F C O Y X T M O Y M L O Q A Q N J T
E P I C P T U Z U H B H V X Y D V H P B
```

1. Playmaker

2. Barcelona

3. Striker

4. Champions League

5. Camp Nou

6. La Liga

7. Dribbler

8. PSG

9. Copa America

10. Copa Del Rey

BREAKTHROUGH AT BARCELONA

"Messi is a god, as a person and even more as a player. I knew him when he was a boy and I've watched him grow. He deserves it all."

- Samuel Eto'o

10 Trivia Answers

Lionel Messi debuted for Barcelona's senior team as a second half substitute in a November 2003 friendly against former Barcelona assistant manager, Jose Mourinho's FC Porto. He created two chances and had a shot on goal during his 15-minute cameo, to the delight of Barcelona technical staff. He subsequently began having his daily training sessions with Barcelona B, and a weekly session with the first team. Ronaldinho, recently recruited from PSG, told his teammates he believed Messi would mature into a much better player than himself.

Messi's progress was rewarded with a first professional contract, signed in February 2004 with a length of 8 years and an initial buyout clause of 30 million euros, which rose to 80 million euros automatically following his debut for the reserves. In October 2004, he was promoted to the first team by then Barcelona manager, Frank Rijkaard, on the request of senior first team players.

Messi made his competitive debut on 16 October 2004, coming on as an 82nd minute substitute for Deco in a La Liga match against Espanyol. Being 17 years, three months, and 22 days old at the time, Messi became Barcelona's youngest ever player in a competitive fixture. He racked up 244 minutes in 9 substitute appearances for the first team during the course of the 2004/05 season and scored his first senior goal on 1 May 2005 in a La Liga fixture against Albacete, becoming at the time, Barcelona's youngest ever goalscorer in an official competition. He celebrated the first major trophy of his career when Barcelona lifted the La Liga title a few weeks later.

Messi was rewarded with his first contract as a first team player on 24 June 2005, his 18th birthday. It had a duration of 5 years and contained a buyout clause of 150 million euros. He was named in the starting lineup for the first time against Juventus in the Joan Gamper Trophy, Barcelona's preseason tournament. His impressive performance earned him a standing ovation from the Camp Nou, and exultant commendation from then Juventus manager, Fabio Capello, who wanted to take Messi to Juventus on loan. Juventus' fierce rivals, Inter Milan, also offered to pay his release clause and triple his wages, but he turned down their advances to remain at Barcelona, where he was offered a second contract renewal in three months, extending his stay until 2014.

Messi missed the start of the 2005/06 season due to issues surrounding his legal status in the Royal Spanish Football Federation (RFEF). He became eligible to play after acquiring Spanish citizenship on 26 September. He was handed the number 19 jersey after he had worn number 30 in his first couple of seasons with the first team, and he gradually established himself as Barcelona's first choice right-winger in a fearsome attacking triumvirate that included Samuel Eto'o and Ronaldinho.

Messi was named in the starting lineup for key matches, like his first *Clasico*, at the home of fierce rivals Real Madrid in November 2005, and Barcelona's UEFA Champions League Round of 16 first leg game at Chelsea in February 2006. He scored 8 goals in 25 competitive fixtures before his season ended abruptly after he suffered a torn hamstring in the second leg of the Champions League tie against Chelsea. He did not celebrate Barcelona's UEFA Champions League final victory over Arsenal in May 2006 due to the disappointment of playing no part in it.

Despite Barcelona's gradual decline, Messi's upward trajectory as one of the best players in Europe continued. He scored 17 goals in 36 games in all competitions during the 2006/07 season, including a memorable first career hattrick in the *Clasico*. He even replicated two of Diego Maradona's most famous goals, a player he had drawn similar comparisons to, in the latter stages of that season against Getafe and Espanyol. Barcelona endured a second successive season without a major trophy despite Messi's haul of 16 goals in all competitions during the 2007/08 season.

10 Trivia Questions

1. When did Messi play for Barcelona's first team for the first time?

    A. 2002

    B. 2003

    C. 2004

    D. 2005

2. Messi made his competitive debut for Barcelona against_____?

    A. Real Madrid

    B. Osasuna

    C. Espanyol

    D. Ajax

3. Messi played his first UEFA Champions League game against _____?

    A. Shaktar Donetsk

    B. Celtic

    C. Panathinaikos

    D. Lyon

4. Messi's first contract renewal after breaking into the first team had a buyout clause of_____?

   A. 100m euros

   B. 120m euros

   C. 140m euros

   D. 150m euros

5. Messi's first start for Barcelona's first team came against_____?

   A. Inter Milan

   B. Juventus

   C. Roma

   D. AC Milan

6. Which player assisted Messi's first competitive Barcelona goal?

   A. Deco

   B. Eto'o

   C. Ronaldinho

   D. Xavi

7. Messi scored his first official Barcelona goal against_____?

   A. Albacete

   B. Numancia

   C. Real Betis

   D. Villareal

8. When did Messi play in the *Clasico* for the first time?

   A. 2003

   B. 2004

   C. 2005

   D. 2006

9. Messi scored his first Champions League goal against _____?

   A. Lyon

   B. Dynamo Kyiv

   C. Rangers

   D. Panathinaikos

10. Messi scored his first career hattrick against _____?

    A. Celtic

    B. Real Madrid

    C. Valencia

    D. Fenerbahce

Word Scramble #1

1. LAOOTFLB   _____
2. EPLAYNT   _____
3. KCFRKIEE   _____
4. OOAZGL   _____
5. ELBIRBRD   _____
6. YKRMAAPEL   _____
7. DTTFOEFELO   _____
8. NOAELRABC   _____
9. PIRSA   _____
10. ROFRDAW   _____

GLORY YEARS AT BARCELONA

"One day I will tell my grandchildren that I trained Leo Messi. With Messi you have to speak to him in small doses and listen carefully to the little that he says. Don't write about him, don't try to understand how he does it, just watch him."

- Pep Guardiola

Following the departure of manager Frank Rijkaard and superstar players Ronaldinho and Deco ahead of the start of the 2008/09 season, Messi was made Barcelona's highest paid player and given the number 10 shirt. The club also implemented new training, nutrition, and lifestyle routines, and paired Messi up with a personal physiotherapist that accompanied him on international duty call-ups, all in a bid to combat his frequent muscular injuries. Messi remained injury-free for most of the next 4 years and had an incredible first season under Pep Guardiola, scoring 38 goals in 51 games to help Barcelona to a treble of La Liga, Copa del Rey, and UEFA Champions League.

Messi was made the focal point of Barcelona's attack halfway into the 2009/10 season, despite the expensive acquisition of Swedish striker Zlatan Ibrahimović in the previous summer. Messi scored 47 times in all competitions, matching Ronaldo's club record set in 1996/97 as Barcelona retained the La Liga title. Messi also finished as Champions League top goalscorer for a second successive season with 8 goals, and La Liga top goalscorer with 34 goals, a tally that earned him his first European Golden Shoe.

Messi began the 2010/11 season with a hattrick in a 4-0 home victory that secured Barcelona the Supercopa de Espana against Sevilla, after Barcelona lost the first leg. It was also his hattrick against Atletico Madrid in February 2011 that secured Barcelona a 3-0 win and a Spanish top flight record of 16 consecutive wins.

Messi scored 3 goals in 4 *Clasico* matches played towards the end of the 2010/11 season, including a brace in a 2-0 win at Real Madrid in the UEFA Champions League semifinal first leg. He finished the season on 53 goals in all competitions and helped Barcelona capture a third straight La Liga title and a second Champions League trophy in three seasons.

Messi's offensive capabilities continued to improve, combining lethal finishing with intricate bits of playmaking to rack up more than 100 goal involvements during the 2011/12 season, scoring 73 goals and providing 29 assists in 60 club games. Barcelona witnessed a decline in fortunes, winning only the Copa del Rey in Guardiola's final season, but Messi set a single season record for most La Liga goals (50), and most goals in European club football (73). He also surpassed Cesar Rodriguez's haul of 232 goals to become Barcelona's all-time highest goalscorer with a hattrick against Granada, and became the first player to score 5 goals in a UEFA Champions League game in a 7-1 rout of Bayer Leverkusen.

Now playing under his former *La Masia* coach, Tito Vilanova, Messi helped Barcelona to their best ever start to a La Liga season, amassing a Spanish top flight record of 55 points from the first 19 rounds of fixtures.

He became Barcelona's all-time highest goalscorer in La Liga with a brace against Real Betis that took him past Cesar Rodriguez's haul of 190, and broke Gerd Muller's 40-year-old record for most goals in a single calendar year with 91 goals in 2012, six goals clear of Muller's record of 85. Messi captained Barcelona for the first time in a league game against Rayo Vallecano March 2013 as they clinched the title with 100 points, equaling Real Madrid's record from the previous season.

Despite an injury-plagued 2013, Messi scored in a world record 21 successive league fixtures, scoring 33 goals in the course of that run and becoming the first player to score against the entire 19 La Liga opponents consecutively. He finished the 2012/13 season with 46 league goals to pick up a third *Pichichi* and also become the first player to win three European Golden Shoes.

Former Newell's Old Boys manager, Gerardo Martino, was handed the reins at Barcelona ahead of the start of the 2013/14 season, as Messi continued to be plagued by muscular problems, suffering a fifth injury of 2013 in November and spending two months on the sidelines. He scored 41 goals in all competitions by the end of the season but Barcelona missed out on a major trophy for the first time in six seasons.

Messi had a mostly injury-free 2014/15 season under the tutelage of former club captain, Luis Enrique. He formed a formidable attacking triumvirate with Neymar and summer recruit Luis Suarez, dubbed "MSN," to replicate Barcelona's treble success from six years prior. Messi broke Telmo Zarra's record of 251 Spanish top flight goals, and finished the season with 58 goals in all competitions.

Messi picked up from where he left off in the previous season, scoring two freekicks in Barcelona's 5-4 extra time victory over Sevilla in the 2015 UEFA Super Cup. He became the youngest player to reach 100 Champions League appearances in Barcelona's first group game at Roma, and rounded off the year by lifting a fifth club trophy of 2015 following Barcelona's win over River Plate in the FIFA Club World Cup final. Messi assisted both goals in Barcelona's extra time victory over Sevilla in the Copa del Rey final to help Barcelona secure the domestic double for a second straight season.

Messi began the 2016/17 campaign by lifting the Supercopa de Espana in the absence of substantive captain, Andres Iniesta, following Barcelona's 5-0 aggregate victory over Sevilla. In his first Champions League match of 2016/17, Messi scored a sixth Champions League hattrick in Barcelona's 7-0 rout of Celtic, and surpassed Raul Gonzalez's record of 53 goals in the Champions League group stage when he scored his 54th in a 3-1 defeat at Manchester City. Messi scored 54 goals in all competitions, including one in the Copa del Rey final win over Alaves that secured Barcelona a third successive Copa del Rey title, after narrowly missing out on La Liga by three points.

Messi's penalty proved too little as Barcelona lost the first leg of the 2017 Supercopa de Espana to Real Madrid, with the second leg also finishing 2-0 in favour of the capital-based side. Messi scored the fastest goal of his career, finding the back of the net 2 minutes and 8 seconds into Barcelona's 3-0 win over Chelsea in March 2018, and finished the league season on 34 goals to pick up both *Pichichi* and European Golden Shoe for the fifth time in his career. He also had a goal and assist in Barcelona's fourth successive Copa del Rey final triumph, thrashing Sevilla 5-0 to complete the league and cup domestic double.

Ahead of the start of the 2018/19 campaign, Messi was made Barcelona captain following the departure of Andres Iniesta at the end of the previous season. Messi lifted the 2018 Supercopa de Espana, his first trophy as permanent Barcelona captain following a 2-1 win over Sevilla. In late April, he came off the bench to score the only goal of Barcelona's home win over Levante that clinched the league title for his side. He scored 51 goals in all competitions, 36 of those coming in the league to draw level with Telmo Zarra on 6 Spanish top flight top scorer awards and also claim a record-extending sixth European Golden Shoe.

Messi missed Barcelona's United States tour in August 2019 due to a calf injury, and did not make his first appearance of the 2019/20 season until 17 September. Messi finished as top scorer and assister in La Liga with 26 goals and 21 assists respectively. He claimed a record seventh *Pichichi*, but missed out on a major trophy and suffered the heaviest defeat of his career in Barcelona's aggregate 8-2 defeat at the hands of Bayern Munich in the Champions League.

Amid growing discontent with Barcelona's deteriorating state on and off the pitch, the club revealed that they had received a document from Messi which expressed the star forward's intention to leave the club on 25 August 2020. The club reiterated their desire to build a team around Messi and warned off any potential suitors with the 700 million euros buyout clause in his contract, although he could have left for free if he had communicated his intent three months earlier, as stated in the contract.

Messi ultimately decided to remain at Barcelona for one final season, instead of going to court against his beloved club. He was sent off for the first time in his club career during Barcelona's 3-2 loss to Athletic Bilbao in the 2020/21 Supercopa de Espana semifinal but scored twice against the same opponents to help Barcelona win 4-0 in the 2021 Copa del Rey final. In what turned out to be his last game for Barcelona, Messi scored his 30th league goal of the season in a 2-1 loss to Celta Vigo, finishing the season as top scorer and claiming a record-extending eighth *Pichichi* trophy.

10 Trivia Questions

1. How many goals were scored by Messi in the 2008/09 season for Barcelona?

    A. 38

    B. 45

    C. 23

    D. 41

2. How many goals did Messi score in Barcelona's 6-2 win at Real Madrid in May 2009?

    A. 0

    B. 1

    C. 2

    D. 4

3. Who were the opponents when Messi played in his first cup final for Barcelona?

    A. Real Madrid

    B. Athletic Bilbao

    C. Atletico Madrid

    D. Real Betis

4. How many Champions League goals did Messi finish with in the 2008/09 season?

   A. 6

   B. 7

   C. 8

   D. 9

5. Messi scored 4 goals in a match for the first time against _____?

   A. Arsenal

   B. Porto

   C. Atletico Madrid

   D. Rubin Kazan

6. How many league goals won Messi his first European Golden Shoe?

   A. 25

   B. 34

   C. 38

   D. 43

7. How many goals did Messi score in Barcelona's 5-0 win over Real Madrid in November 2010?

   A. 3

   B. 2

   C. 1

   D. 0

8. Messi became Barcelona's all-time highest goalscorer after a hattrick against_____?

   A. Girona

   B. Granada

   C. Levante

   D. Malaga

9. How many hat-tricks were scored by Messi in the 2011/12 season?

    A. 7

    B. 10

    C. 5

    D. 2

10. Messi scored his last goal for Barcelona against_____?

    A. Elche

    B. Eibar

    C. Celta Vigo

    D. Alaves

10 Trivia Answers

1. A – 38

2. C – 2

3. B – Athletic Bilbao

4. D – 9

5. A – Arsenal

6. B – 34

7. D – 0

8. B – Granada

9. B – 10

10. C – Celta Vigo

Start

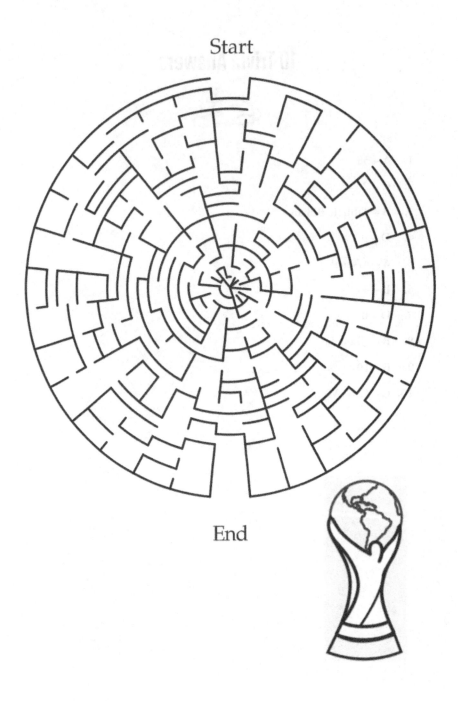

End

TRANSFER TO PSG

"I have fun like a child in the street. When the day comes when I'm not enjoying it, I will leave football."

- Lionel Messi

Messi became a free agent on July 1st, 2021 as Barcelona could not renew his contract due to the dire financial state of the Catalan club. He joined Paris Saint-Germain (PSG) on 10 August 2021, penning a 2-year deal with an optional third year, and chose jersey number 30, the same he wore nearly two decades previously when he first played for Barcelona's senior team.

Messi debuted for PSG in a 2-0 Ligue 1 win at Reims in late August, and made his first Champions League appearance and first start in a 1-1 draw at Club Brugge in the middle of September. He made his first home appearance in a 2-1 win over Lyon on 19 September, and scored his first PSG goal in a 2-0 Champions League win over Pep Guardiola's Manchester City on 28 September. He scored his first Ligue 1 goal in a 3-1 win over Nantes at PSG's Parc de Princes home ground on 21 November, and provided a hattrick of assists in a single game for the fifth time in his career in PSG's 3-1 win at Saint-Etienne at the end of November.

Having missed PSG's first 3 games of 2022 due to illness, Messi marked his return to the side with an assist in a 4-0 home win over Reims on 23 January. Following PSG's elimination at the hands of Real Madrid in the Champions League Round of 16, Messi and Neymar were booed by some sections of fans in the home game against Bordeaux, but Messi was staunchly defended by PSG manager Mauricio Pochettino, citing his incomplete readjustment among reasons for his perceived ineffectiveness.

Messi helped PSG clinch a tenth Ligue 1 title on 23 April, scoring a goal from distance in a 1-1 draw at home against Lens. He finished the season with just 6 league goals, failing to reach double figures for the first time since 2005/06, and a total of 11 goals and 14 assists in all competitions.

Messi began his second season at PSG playing in his preferred free role under new manager Christophe Galtier. He scored his side's first goal in a 4-0 win over Nantes on 31 July, securing the *Trophee des Champions* and his second piece of silverware with PSG. He assisted Mbappe's goal, the second fastest in Ligue 1 history, and scored one himself in PSG's 7-1 win at Lille on 21 August, and was named Ligue 1 Player of the Month in September thanks to 1 goal and 5 assists. He became the first player to score against 40 different teams in the Champions League following his strike in a 1-1 draw at Benfica on 5 October. In a 7-2 win over Maccabi Haifa in the same competition on 25 October, he scored his 22nd and 23rd Champions

League goals from outside the 18-yard box to set a new record for goals scored from that range. Messi beat his goals tally from his first season, with his strike in PSG's 4-3 win against Troyes at the end of October being his 7th in the league and 12th in all competitions.

10 Trivia Questions

1. How much did PSG pay to acquire the services of Lionel Messi?

    A. 50m euros

    B. 150m euros

    C. 100m euros

    D. Free transfer

2. Which jersey number did Messi pick on arrival at PSG?

    A. 10

    B. 19

    C. 30

    D. 28

3. Messi completed his move to PSG in the month of_____?

    A. September

    B. August

    C. July

    D. June

4. How long was Messi's first PSG contract to last?

    A. 2

    B. 3

    C. 4

    D. 5

5. Messi made his PSG debut against_____?

   A. Rennes

   B. Manchester City

   C. Monaco

   D. Reims

6. Messi made his PSG home debut against_____?

   A. Marseille

   B. Monaco

   C. Lyon

   D. Benfica

7. In which of these competitions did Messi score his first goal for PSG?

   A. Trophee des Champions

   B. UEFA Champions League

   C. Ligue 1

   D. Coupe de France

8. Messi provided 3 assists in a win for PSG against _____?

   A. Saint Etienne

   B. Lens

   C. Nantes

   D. Strasbourg

9. Messi's first PSG goal was scored against_____?

   A. Lyon

   B. Reims

   C. Club Brugge

   D. Manchester City

10. Messi scored his first league goal for PSG against_____?

    A. Reims

    B. Lyon

    C. Nantes

    D. Lorient

10 Trivia Answers

1. D – Free transfer

2. C – 30

3. B – August

4. A – 2

5. D – Reims

6. C – Lyon

7. B – UEFA Champions League

8. A – Saint Etienne

9. D – Manchester City

10. C – Nantes

1. KZKHFZ _____
2. JCM _____
3. EMJYXM _____
4. ORF _____
5. YXOZBILKX _____

6. TBK _____
7. ODMZKSX _____
8. BZLOMNT _____
9. SCDY _____
10. JBPPF _____

A. Penalty   B. Barcelona   C. Golazo   D. UCL

E. La Liga   F. UEFA   G. PSG

H. Leo   I. Messi   J. Camp Nou

INTERNATIONAL CAREER

*"I think he reached and surpassed the level of Maradona.
He does incredible things, at a speed that is insane."*

- Paolo Maldini

Messi was eligible to represent either Argentina or Spain at international level as he had citizenship status in both countries. He turned down Spain's approach when approached by under-17 selectors in 2003, as he had aspirations of representing his country of birth since childhood.

He made his debut for Argentina under-20 in a friendly against Paraguay on 29 June 2004, scoring a goal and providing two assists in an 8-0 win, and subsequently made the squad for the 2005 South American under-20 youth Championship held in Colombia in February 2005. He made six appearances as a substitute and scored the winning goal against Brazil that secured his team third-place and qualification for the 2005 FIFA World Youth Championship.

Messi did not start Argentina's first game at the 2005 FIFA World Youth Championship, which his team eventually lost 1-0 to USA, but started every other game from then onwards, and scored a brace in the final against Nigeria to claim Argentina's sixth title and earn himself both the Golden Ball and Golden Boot.

Messi made his senior debut on 17 August 2005 in a friendly exhibition against Hungary, coming on as a second half substitute. He lasted on the pitch for just two minutes however, as he was sent off for a foul on Hungary's Vilmos Vanczak. He made another cameo appearance in the 2006 World Cup qualifier against Paraguay in September, and was handed a first start in the next qualifier against Peru, where he won a penalty that secured his side a crucial win. He received regular call-ups for the games leading up to Argentina's World Cup campaign in June 2006, scoring his first goal in a March 2006 friendly against Croatia.

After he was left on the bench for the entirety of Argentina's 2006 World Cup opening game against Cote d'Ivoire, Messi was introduced in the 74th minute of the second game against Serbia & Montenegro, becoming Argentina's youngest player at the World Cup and sixth youngest goalscorer in World Cup history when he netted the last goal in a 6-0 rout. With progression to the next round secured after two games, Messi started the final group game that ended in a goalless draw against the Netherlands, and was brought on after 84 minutes in the Round of 16 extra time victory over Mexico. He played no part in Argentina's penalty shootout defeat against Germany, following a 1-1 draw at the end of extra time.

Messi had developed into one of the best players in the world by the time the 2007 Copa America came around, and he played an instrumental role in Argentina's run to the final that eventually resulted in a 3-0 defeat to Brazil. Barcelona sought to prevent him from representing Argentina at the 2008 Summer Olympics Football Event, but the club changed their stance following the intervention of new manager Pep Guardiola. Messi was one of Argentina's best players at the tournament, as his goal and assist secured a hard-fought victory over the Netherlands in the quarterfinal, before he set up the winner against Nigeria in the gold medal match.

Messi scored four goals in Argentina's qualification campaign for the 2010 World Cup, and was handed the number 10 shirt in March 2009, following the retirement of Juan Roman Riquelme. Argentina were considered as one of the favourites for the 2010 World Cup despite their underwhelming qualifying campaign. They started the tournament brilliantly, winning all three group games against Nigeria, South Korea, and Greece. As was the case four years earlier, Germany ended Argentina's dream in the quarterfinal. Messi was heavily criticized by Argentina fans for his failure to replicate his match-winning performances for Barcelona with the national team.

Argentina's 2008 Olympic Gold Medal-winning coach, Sergio Batista, replaced Diego Maradona and vowed to build a team around Messi, deploying the then Barcelona forward as a false striker in a 4-3-3. The plan did not turn out as effective as he had hoped, as Messi's goal drought in international official matches dragged on through the entirety of the 2011 Copa America, where Argentina bowed out in the quarterfinal to eventual winners, Uruguay.

Messi was made Argentina captain in August 2011 by Alejandro Sabella, who had replaced Sergio Batista following Argentina's underwhelming outing at the 2011 Copa America. Messi ended his goal drought in official international matches on 7 October against Chile, Argentina's first 2014 World Cup qualifying match. He became more prolific under Sabella, scoring a remarkable 25 goals in 32 games, in stark contrast to just 17 goals in 61 matches under all the previous Argentina national team managers he had worked with.

Messi scored his first international hattrick against Switzerland on 29 February 2012, and matched Gabriel Batistuta's national record of 12 goals in a calendar year by the end of 2012. He scored two further hattricks against Guatemala and Brazil over the course of the following 18 months, and helped Argentina seal qualification for the 2014 World Cup with a brace in a 5-2 win over Paraguay in September 2013. Those two goals moved him up to second as Argentina's second highest goalscorer with 37 goals, and he finished the qualification campaign with 10 goals in 14 appearances.

Messi went into the 2014 World Cup off the back of a trophy-less and injury-ravaged season with Barcelona, leading many to doubt both his form and state of mind. However, he started the tournament strongly, and was named Man of the Match in each of his side's first 4 games, scoring 4 goals in group stage wins against Bosnia & Herzegovina, Iran, and Nigeria, and providing the assist for the winner in extra time against Switzerland in the Round of 16. He played in the 1-0 win over Belgium in the quarterfinal, and scored his side's first penalty in the shootout victory over the Netherlands in the semifinal. In a repeat of what transpired 24 years back, Argentina lost the final 1-0 to Germany, with the only goal of the game coming off the boot of substitute Mario Gotze seven minutes from the end of extra time. Messi was awarded the Golden Ball as the tournament's best player, but the decision drew a lot of criticism due to his lack of goals in the knockout phase.

Messi became the fifth Argentine player to reach 100 caps in his team's final group game against Jamaica at the 2015 Copa America. He had scored a penalty in the 2-2 draw against Paraguay in the first group game, and played in the second group game that finished in a 1-0 win over Uruguay. Messi scored his side's first spot kick in the shootout victory over Colombia in the quarterfinal, and provided 3 assists in the 6-1 rout of Paraguay in the semifinal. He was also the only Argentina player that converted his penalty in the 4-1 shootout defeat to Chile after the final had ended goalless.

Due to fitness concerns, Messi missed Argentina's 2-1 win over holders Chile in their first group game at the 2016 Copa America Centenario. He scored a hattrick in 19 minutes and was named Man of the Match after coming on as a second half substitute in the second game against Panama. He provided two assists and scored a goal that drew him level with Gabriel Batistuta on 54 Argentina goals in a 4-1 win over Venezuela in the quarterfinal. Messi became Argentina's all-time highest goalscorer in another Man of the Match performance against USA in the semifinal, scoring from a freekick and providing two assists to help Argentina reach a second straight Copa America final. In a repeat of the showpiece from a year ago, Argentina lost on penalties to Chile after a goalless draw, with Messi missing his spot kick in the shootout on this occasion. He announced his retirement from the national team immediately after the game.

Messi reversed his decision to quit international football following pleas from prominent political figures, footballers, and fans, in Argentina. He scored in his first game back, the only goal of a 1-0 win over Uruguay in a 2018 World Cup qualifier on 1 September. Messi sealed Argentina's place at the 2018 World Cup with a hattrick in a 3-1 comeback win over Ecuador in the final round of qualifying games to become the joint-highest goalscorer in CONMEBOL World Cup qualifiers, tied with Uruguayan striker and then Barcelona teammate, Luis Suarez on 21 goals.

Messi spurned a chance to give Argentina all 3 points, missing a penalty in their 1-1 draw with Iceland in their first game at the 2018 World Cup. Messi was subdued for much of Argentina's 3-0 loss to Croatia in the second game, before his brace helped beat Nigeria 2-1 and earn his side a spot in the Round of 16, where they crashed out following a 4-3 defeat to eventual winners France.

Messi pulled out of Argentina duty for the remainder of 2018 and seriously considered retiring, before he was convinced to stay on by his idol, Pablo Aimar, and new Argentina coach, Lionel Scaloni. He returned to the team in a March 2019 friendly against Venezuela, and was subsequently named in Argentina's 2019 Copa America squad. He scored his only goal at the tournament in a 1-1 draw against Paraguay in the second group game, and received intense criticism for his performance in the 2-0 quarterfinal win over Venezuela. Argentina were eliminated in the semifinal following a 2-0 loss to eventual champions Brazil.

In the 2019 *Superclasico de las Americas* match against Brazil played in November 2019, Messi scored the rebound from his saved penalty to hand Argentina a 1-0 win, and also scored the only goal that gave Argentina a 1-0 win over Ecuador in their first 2022 World Cup qualifier in October 2020.

Messi scored from a freekick in Argentina's opening game of the 2021 Copa America, and drew level with Javier Mascherano as the joint-most capped player for Argentina with his 147th cap in a 1-0 win over Paraguay. On the day Messi became Argentina's most capped player, he scored twice and provided an assist in a 4-1 win over Bolivia. He scored once and provided three assists in wins over Ecuador and Colombia to help Argentina reach the final, where they defeated Brazil 1-0 courtesy of Angel di Maria's first half goal. Messi lifted his first major international title and picked up the Golden Boot. He also shared the player of the tournament award with Brazil's Neymar.

Messi's hattrick in a 3-0 win over Bolivia in a 2022 World Cup qualifier moved him ahead of Pele as South America's all-time highest goalscorer in men's international football with 79 goals. He also set up two of Argentina's goals in a 3-0 win over Italy in the *Finalissima*, the third edition of the UEFA-CONMEBOL Cup of Champions, and scored all five goals in a 5-0 win over Estonia in a warm-up game ahead of the 2022 World Cup.

Messi scored Argentina's first goal at the 2022 World Cup, converting a penalty in a surprise 2-1 loss to Saudi Arabia. He scored one and set up the other in a 2-0 win over Mexico in the second game, and played in the 2-0 win over Poland in the last group game. Messi scored the first goal of Argentina's 2-1 win over Australia in the Round of 16, and provided an assist for the first goal before scoring the second in a 2-2 draw against the Netherlands in the quarterfinal, with Argentina advancing to the semifinal following a 4-3 victory in the shootout. Messi had another Man of the Match performance in the semifinal, with a goal and assist in a 3-0 win over Croatia.

Messi declared that the final against France, a record 26th World Cup appearance for him, would be his last ever World Cup match. He scored twice in an absorbing game that finished 3-3 after extra time, and converted his team's first spot kick in a penalty shootout that his side edged 4-2.

Messi lifted his country's first World Cup in 36 years and claimed a second Golden Ball. He also surpassed Pele as the player with the most goal involvements in World Cup history with 21 (13 goals and 8 assists). Messi confirmed that he was not retiring from international football yet, as he wished to "continue playing as a champion."

10 Trivia Questions

1. Messi made his senior international debut against _____?

    A. Bulgaria

    B. Hungary

    C. Romania

    D. Belgium

2. Messi scored his first senior international goal against_____?

    A. Serbia

    B. Nigeria

    C. Croatia

    D. Brazil

3. How many appearances did Messi make at the 2006 World Cup?

    A. 5

    B. 2

    C. 1

    D. 3

4. At which year's Summer Olympics did Messi win gold in the football event?

    A. 2008

    B. 2012

    C. 2004

    D. 2000

5. In which of these World Cup editions did Messi not score a goal?

    A.   2006 World Cup

    B.   2010 World Cup

    C.   2014 World Cup

    D.   2018 World Cup

6. Who did Messi score his first international hattrick against?

    A.   Paraguay

    B.   Guatemala

    C.   Switzerland

    D.   Brazil

7. Who were the opponents when Messi scored his first World Cup goal?

    A.   Mexico

    B.   Iran

    C.   Nigeria

    D.   Serbia & Montenegro

8. Messi's first goal in the knockout stage of the World Cup came against
    _____?

    A.   Australia

    B.   France

    C.   Netherlands

    D.   Mexico

9. Messi won his 100th international cap in a game against_____?

    A.   Paraguay

    B.   Jamaica

    C.   Colombia

    D.   Uruguay

10. On the day Messi became Argentina's all-time highest goalscorer, who were the opponents?

   A. Chile

   B. Venezuela

   C. USA

   D. Panama

10 Trivia Answers

1. B – Hungary

2. C – Croatia

3. D – 3

4. A – 2008

5. B – 2010 World Cup

6. C – Switzerland

7. D – Serbia & Montenegro

8. A – Australia

9. B – Jamaica

10. C – USA

Messi Crossword #1

Unscramble the letters to solve the puzzle!

ACROSS

[1] Messi's first coach at Barcelona

[3] Messi's first club

[4] Messi's biggest trophy

[5] Messi's strong foot

[6] Messi's nationality

[8] Messi's trio in 2015

[9] Messi's number in PSG

DOWN

[1] Assisted Messi's first goal

[2] Messi's middle name

[7] Messi's Brazilian friend

PROFILE & STYLE OF PLAY

"Messi does not need his right foot. He only uses the left and he's still the best in the world. Imagine if he also used his right foot, then we would have serious problems."

- Zlatan Ibrahimovic

D ue to his diminutive stature, Messi has a reduced centre of gravity in comparison to taller footballers. This enhances his agility and allows him to switch directions and avoid tackles easily, earning him the nickname *La Pulga Atomica* or "The Atomic Flea" from the Spanish press.

Despite his physical limitation, Messi possesses appreciable upper-body strength, which combined with his diminished centre of gravity and commensurate poise helps him withstand heavy challenges from opposing players, earning him plaudits for not going to ground too easily in a game filled with playacting. His nimble feet allow him to get away quickly from opponents and retain possession of the ball while dribbling at speed, leading to his former Barcelona manager Pep Guardiola's assertion that 'Messi is the only player that runs faster with the ball than he does without it."

Messi is predominantly left-footed, although his ability with his weaker right foot has improved tremendously over the course of his career. He normally starts dribbling runs with the outside of his left foot, while he utilizes the inside of his left foot to finish chances or supply passes and assists. He seldom uses his right foot for anything other than finishing off chances.

Messi has carved for himself a reputation as a prolific goalscorer. He is renowned for his finishing, quick reactions, positioning, and ability to make clever offensive runs to beat opposing defensive lines. He also excels in a playmaking role, thanks to his accuracy, vision, and range of passing. He has been repeatedly described as a magician, wizard, or conjurer, creating goals and chances from the most unlikely scenarios. He is also notable for his accuracy from penalty kicks and freekicks, and he is ranked a respectable ninth in all-time goals scored from freekicks with 60 strikes as of October 2022.

He also has a strong inclination to scoring chipped goals when faced with onrushing goalkeepers. Besides his astonishing individual qualities, Messi is also an accomplished, versatile, and committed team player, well-known for his creative combinations, particularly with former Barcelona midfielders Andres Iniesta and Xavier Hernandez.

Messi operates in a free attacking role, his versatility enabling him to be deployed on either wing on through the middle of the pitch. His most preferred position growing up was as a playmaker behind two strikers, a role referred to as *enganche* in Argentina, but he started off in Spain as a left-sided forward or left winger.

After he broke into the first team, then Barcelona coach Frank Rijkaard shifted him to the right wing, from where he can cut into the centre of pitch on his favoured left foot and shoot at goal, rather than mostly crossing the ball to teammates from the left wing. He was utilized as a false nine under Pep Guardiola and most of the managers who came after him, with Messi positioned as a centre forward and given freedom to roam the central positions, sometimes dragging defenders out of place by dropping deep into midfield so as to open gaps in opposition defenses for his teammates to exploit.

As Messi's career peaked and his ability to explosively dribble somewhat diminished, he adopted a more creative role, setting the pace from deeper sections of the pitch and developing into one of the game's greatest passers and playmakers. His work-rate out of possession and defensive contributions also diminished as his career advanced, covering less ground on the field and saving his energy only for short runs. This improved his efficiency, movement, positioning, and also helped him avoid the muscular injuries that plagued the early part of his career.

Messi has played in various positions along the frontline under different managers while on international duty with the Argentine national team. He has been utilized as a right winger, as a false nine, as a lone striker, as a supporting striker alongside another forward, or in a deep, free creative role as a prototype number 10 playmaker or attacking midfielder behind two strikers. Messi also looks up and points his index fingers to the sky when celebrating a goal, a tribute to his grandmother who discovered his talent and set him on the path to becoming arguably the greatest footballer of all-time.

10 Trivia Questions

1. How tall is Lionel Messi?

    A. 170 cm

    B. 175 cm

    C. 180 cm

    D. 165 cm

2. How many freekick goals has Messi scored in his career (February 2023)?

    A. 40

    B. 50

    C. 60

    D. 70

3. Which trait enables Messi to get away easily from opponents?

    A. Nimble feet

    B. Aerial prowess

    C. Fierce ball-striking

    D. Full head of hair

4. How many headed goals has Messi scored in his career (February 2023)?

    A. 19

    B. 28

    C. 32

    D. 24

5. Messi predominantly uses his right foot to_____?

   A. Pass

   B. Dribble

   C. Cross

   D. Finish chances

6. 'Messi is the only player that runs faster with the ball than he does without it" was a statement made by_____?

   A. Gerardo Martino

   B. Pep Guardiola

   C. Lionel Scaloni

   D. Tito Vilanova

7. Messi's preferred playmaking role is known in Argentina as _____?

   A. Panache

   B. Apache

   C. Enganche

   D. Gauche

8. Messi began his career in Spain playing as a _____?

   A. Left winger

   B. Right winger

   C. Attacking midfielder

   D. Centre forward

9. Messi appeared to use his hand to score a goal in 2007 against_____?

   A. Getafe

   B. Sevilla

   C. Osasuna

   D. Espanyol

10. Messi looks up and points to the sky when celebrating a goal as a tribute to his_____?

    A. Cousin

    B. Grandmother

    C. Grandfather

    D. Friend

10 Trivia Answers

1. A – 170 cm

2. C – 60

3. A – Nimble feet

4. D – 24

5. D – Finish chances

6. B – Pep Guardiola

7. C – Enganche

8. A – Left winger

9. D – Espanyol

10. B – Grandmother

Start

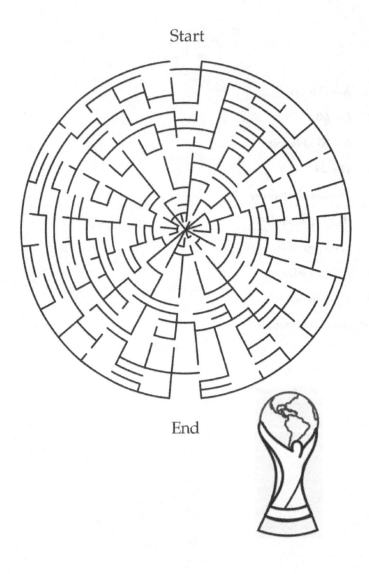

End

CAREER ACHIEVEMENTS

"Messi will be the player to win the most Ballons d'Or in history. He will win five, six, seven. He is incomparable. He's in a different league."

- Johan Cruyff

Lionel Messi has won almost every team and individual accolade to lend credence to the argument of many football enthusiasts that he is indeed the greatest footballer of all-time. His 35 trophies with Barcelona single him out as the most decorated plyer at a single football club. With the exception of the *Coupe de France*, he has won every tournament he has ever contested in his senior career at both club and international level.

Messi has won the coveted *Ballon d'Or* a record seven times, FIFA World Player of the Year once, The Best FIFA Men's Player twice, and the European Golden Shoe a record six times. He is the only player to receive the FIFA World Cup Golden Ball twice, and has also won two Golden Balls at the FIFA Club World Cup, and both the Golden Ball and Golden Boot when he helped Argentina to the FIFA World Youth Championship in 2005.

Messi is Argentina's all-time highest goalscorer and most capped player. He is also the most prolific player in the history of the Spanish top flight, with 474 goals in 520 appearances. He has been named La Liga Best Player 6 times, and he has won the *Pichichi* award for La Liga top scorer a record 8 times. Messi has scored 796 senior career goals for club and country, including 56 hattricks, and has provided 350 assists, the most recorded in football history.

Messi holds the record for most goals scored in a calendar year (91 in 2012), most matches played at the FIFA World Cup (26), most minutes played at the FIFA World Cup (2,314), most FIFA World Cup matches scored in (11), most competitive goals for a single club (672 for Barcelona), most goals and assists in finals (33 & 14 respectively), most appearances in FIFA-FIFPRO World XI (15, from 2007-2021), most FIFA World Cup appearances as captain (19), most FIFA World Cup assists (8), most Man of the Match awards at a single FIFA World Cup (5), most Player of the Match awards in FIFA World Cup history (11), and a host of other plaudits too numerous to mention.

10 Trivia Questions

1. How many trophies has Messi won in his senior career (February 2023)?

    A. 38

    B. 37

    C. 40

    D. 39

2. How many times has Messi won the European Golden Shoe?

    A. 3

    B. 4

    C. 2

    D. 6

3. How many times has Messi finished as La Liga top scorer?

    A. 8

    B. 2

    C. 4

    D. 5

4. The inaugural FIFA Ballon d'Or was won by Messi in _____?

    A. 2009

    B. 2010

    C. 2011

    D. 2012

5. How many appearances has Messi made at the FIFA World Cup?

    A. 24

    B. 15

    C. 26

    D. 32

6. How many "Man of the Match" awards has Messi won in World Cup matches?

    A. 8

    B. 7

    C. 14

    D. 11

7. How many trophies did Messi win at Barcelona?

    A. 35

    B. 34

    C. 33

    D. 32

8. Messi won his first senior international trophy in the year _____?

    A. 2022

    B. 2021

    C. 2020

    D. 2019

9. How many hattricks has Messi scored in his senior career?

    A. 65

    B. 30

    C. 56

    D. 50

10. How many goals has Messi scored in the group stage of the UEFA Champions League?

    A. 75

    B. 76

    C. 77

    D. 78

10 Trivia Answers

1. C – 40

2. D – 6

3. A – 8

4. B – 2010

5. C – 26

6. D – 11

7. A – 35

8. B – 2021

9. C – 56

10. D – 78

1. Striker
2. Lionel
3. Copa America
4. Argentina
5. World Cup
6. Ballon d'Or
7. Dribbler
8. Playmaker

CHAPTER
9

PERSONAL LIFE AND PHILANTHROPY

"Being a bit famous now gives me the opportunity to help people who really need it, especially children."

- Lionel Messi

10 Trivia Questions

1. Messi has been in a relationship with Antonella Roccuzzo since_____?

    A. 2011

    B. 2010

    C. 2009

    D. 2008

2. The tattoo on Messi's left shoulder is of his_____?

    A. Wife

    B. Father

    C. Mother

    D. Sister

3. Antonella Roccuzzo is the cousin of _____?

    A. Hernan Crespo

    B. Lucas Scaglia

    C. Pablo Aimar

    D. Diego Maradona

4. Messi's first son was born in_____?

    A. Barcelona

    B. New York

    C. Paris

    D. London

5. While at FC Barcelona, Messi stayed in_____?

   A. Stiges

   B. Badalona

   C. Terrassa

   D. Castelldefels

6. Which club sent a membership card to Messi's first child?

   A. Barcelona

   B. Grandoli

   C. Newell's Old Boys

   D. PSG

7. One of Messi's favorite dishes is _____?

   A. Chimichurri

   B. Asado

   C. Alfajores

   D. Empanadas

8. Which UN body appointed Messi as a goodwill ambassador?

   A. UNICEF

   B. UNRWA

   C. UNDP

   D. UNEP

9. When was Messi's charitable foundation established?

   A. 2010

   B. 2009

   C. 2008

   D. 2007

10. Which country did Messi visit in his first charitable field mission?

    A. Indonesia

    B. Japan

    C. Haiti

    D. Myanmar

10 Trivia Answers

1. D – 2008

2. C – Mother

3. B – Lucas Scaglia

4. A – Barcelona

5. D – Castelldefels

6. C – Newell's Old Boys

7. B – Asado

8. A – UNICEF

9. D – 2007

10. C – Haiti

Since childhood, Lionel Messi has retained a close relationship with immediate members of his family, especially his mother, Celia, whose face he has emblazoned as a tattoo on his left shoulder. His grandmother, Celia-Oliveira, whose intuition discovered his talent and set him on the path to becoming a world-renowned footballer passed away shortly before his eleventh birthday.

Messi has been in a relationship with Argentine model and fellow Rosario native, Antonella Roccuzzo, since 2008. Messi has known her since he was five years old, as she is the cousin of his childhood best friend, Lucas Scaglia, who is also a professional footballer. Messi kept his relationship with Roccuzzo private for a year, before confirming it in a January 2009 interview, and going public with it a month later, during a carnival in Stiges that followed a Barcelona derby meeting with Espanyol.

Messi has three sons with Antonella Roccuzzo; Thiago, Mateo, and Ciro, born in 2012, 2015 and 2018, respectively. Messi celebrated his partner's first pregnancy by placing the ball under his shirt after he scored in Argentina's 4-0 win over Ecuador in June 2012, and confirmed the pregnancy a fortnight later. Thiago was born on 2 November 2012 in the city of Barcelona. Messi announced that the couple were expecting another child in April 2015. Messi married Roccuzzo on 30 June 2017 in a ceremony held at Hotel City Center in Rosario.

Messi's professional affairs are mostly run like a family business, with his father acting as his agent since his move to Barcelona in 2000. His oldest brother Rodrigo, takes care of his publicity and daily schedules, while his mother and other brother Matias, handle his charitable organization, the Leo Messi foundation, and also manage professional and personal matters in the family's hometown of Rosario in Argentina.

Messi has maintained close ties to his hometown since he departed at the age of 13, and still has that peculiar Rosario accent. He has retained ownership of his family's old house, though it has stayed uninhabited for a long time. He reserves a penthouse apartment in a private residential building for his mother, as well as a family compound in the outskirts of the city. While on international duty with Argentina, he once made a 3-hour trip by road from Buenos Aires to Rosario to have dinner and spend the night with his family, before returning to Buenos Aires for training the following day. He still keeps in touch with a small group of confidants in Rosario, most of whom were also part of "The Machine of 87" at boyhood club Newell's Old Boys.

While playing for FC Barcelona, Messi stayed in Castelldefels, a suburban town in the metropolitan area of the city of Barcelona. His move to Spain from Newell's did not go down well with the Argentine club, but the lengthy public feud ended in 2012, with Newell's sending a club membership card to Messi's first child on the occasion of his birth.

Messi has long-held aspirations to return to Rosario to end his career at the club it began. He has attained citizenship status in Italy, alongside Argentina and Spain, and his favorite dishes include *milanesa, asado,* (traditional South-American barbecue), and pasta, and he likes his *mate* without sugar.

Messi has participated in charitable efforts aimed at improving the living conditions of vulnerable children throughout his career. This commitment may be tied to the health problems he encountered in his own childhood. Since 2004, Messi has spent time and resources at the United Nations Children's Fund (UNICEF), an organization with strong ties to FC Barcelona. He has served as UNICEF goodwill ambassador since his appointment to the role in March 2010, undertaking a maiden field mission a few months later, when he traveled to Haiti for an awareness campaign on the plight of the nation's children in the wake of a devastating earthquake. He has also been involved in UNICEF campaigns on HIV education and prevention, and the social inclusion of children living with disabilities. Messi and his first son, Thiago, participated in a publicity campaign to widen awareness on mortality rates among less-privileged children.

Aside from his work with UNICEF, Messi created his own charitable foundation, the Leo Messi Foundation, which facilitates access to education, health care, and sporting equipment for children. It started in 2007, following Messi's visit to see terminally ill children in a hospital in Boston. Through his organization, he has funded medical training, awarded research grants, and put forth finances for the development of medical centers and projects in Argentina, Spain, and elsewhere on the planet. Aside from his personal fundraising activities like the "Messi and Friends" football exhibitions, his foundation gains financial support from various firms with which he has entered endorsement deals, with Adidas as their chief sponsor.

Messi Crossword #2

Unscramble the letters to solve the puzzle!

ACROSS

[6] Messi's French club

[7] Spanish national league

[9] Barcelona Spanish #5

DOWN

[1] European Cup

[2] Messi's first position

[3] Messi's current position

[4] Barcelona Uruguayan striker

[5] Spanish national cup

[6] Barcelona Spanish #3

[8] Short Spanish center back

ICONIC MOMENTS

*"The other day I saw one of his games. He was running
with the ball at a hundred percent full speed, I don't
know how many touches he took, maybe five or six, but
the ball was glued to his foot. It's practically impossible."*

- Raul

Messi's illustrious career is filled with many awe-inspiring moments. The nimble-footed Argentine made his senior competitive debut for Barcelona on October 16 2004, coming on as an 82nd minute substitute in a La Liga match against local rivals Espanyol. He scored his first competitive goal in a La Liga win over Albacete on 1 May 2005, lifting the ball over Albacete's keeper Raul Valbuena, after receiving a dinked pass from Ronaldinho.

Messi burst onto the global football scene following a string of impressive performances in Argentina's success at the 2005 FIFA World Youth Championship. He was not selected to start Argentina's first game at the tournament, which ended in a 1-0 reverse to the USA. Senior squad players persuaded Francisco Ferraro, the team's coach, to include Messi in the starting 11 as they believed he was the team's best player. Messi scored the first goal in the following game, a 2-0 win over Egypt and had goal involvements in wins over Colombia and Spain in the knockout stage. He was awarded the Golden Ball ahead of the final, in which his two penalties secured the title in a 2-1 victory over Nigeria.

In April 2007, Messi scored the first hattrick of his professional career in an entertaining 3-3 draw against bitter rivals Real Madrid in a La Liga game at Barcelona's Camp Nou stadium. Barcelona went behind three times and Messi pulled them level on each occasion. Around the same period, Messi scored a remarkable solo goal against Getafe, which involved a mazy run from the halfway line, evoking comparisons with compatriot Diego Maradona, who scored a similar goal against England at the 1986 World Cup.

Going into the 2009 UEFA Champions League final between Barcelona and Manchester United, Messi had failed to score in his 10 previous meetings with English teams, leading many to doubt whether he could do it against such caliber of opposition. He put those doubts to rest in spectacular fashion, hanging in the air long enough to meet Xavi's cross from deep with the deftest of touches, a goal he later claimed was the best of his career. Less than a year later, Messi scored all four goals in a 4-1 comeback victory over Arsenal, after the first leg had ended 2-2 in the English capital.

Barcelona faced off with fierce rivals Real Madrid four times in 18 days towards the end of the 2010/11 season. The third game in the series was the first leg of that season's Champions League semifinal at Real's Santiago Bernabeu stadium. The game remained finely poised until the last quarter of an hour when Messi met Ibrahim

Afellay's cross to break the deadlock. Messi did not stop there, as he collected Sergio Busquets' pass inside the center circle, weaved through the Real backline, and slotted a cool finish with the inside of his right foot to put the result beyond doubt. Messi then put in a Man of the Match performance in a repeat of the 2009 final against Manchester United, lashing home the second goal of a 3-1 victory.

Messi scored an incredible 73 club goals in the 2011/12 season, including a record 50 in the Spanish League, and a 5-goal salvo against Bayer Leverkusen in the Champions League Round of 16. Messi finished the year 2012 with an outrageous world record of 91 goals for club and country, deservedly taking home a fourth consecutive Ballon d'Or. He has since collected the prestigious award on three more occasions.

Argentina had slumped to sixth in the CONMEBOL qualifiers for the 2018 World Cup heading into the final round of games after drawing the previous three games. The *Albiceleste* went behind in the first minute of the final game against Ecuador in Quito, before Messi turned the match on its head with two goals to give his side the lead at halftime. His hattrick was complete with a sumptuous chip around the hour mark, ensuring his country's participation at the 2018 World Cup in Russia. His most iconic moment for Argentina came towards the end of 2022, when he led his country to FIFA World Cup glory, scoring in every round and picking up 5 Man of the Match awards along the way. The complete career, at long last!

10 Trivia Questions

1. Which player provided the assist for Messi's first official Barcelona goal?

    A. Eto'o

    B. Giuly

    C. Ronaldinho

    D. Iniesta

2. Messi scored his first career hat-trick in the year _____?

    A. 2008

    B. 2007

    C. 2006

    D. 2005

3. Messi scored five goals in an international match for the first time against_____?

    A. Cameroon

    B. Ecuador

    C. Panama

    D. Estonia

4. Messi scored the first of his 91 goals in 2012 against_____?

   A. Osasuna

   B. Malaga

   C. Real Betis

   D. Levante

5. Messi scored four goals in a game for the first time against _____?

   A. AC Milan

   B. Arsenal

   C. Bayer Leverkusen

   D. Valencia

6. Which player provided the assist for Messi's first goal in a Champions League final?

   A. Eto'o

   B. Henry

   C. Xavi

   D. Iniesta

7. How many *Clasico* hat-tricks did Messi score?

   A. 5

   B. 2

   C. 1

   D. 0

8. When did Messi win his seventh Ballon d'Or _____?

   A. 2018

   B. 2019

   C. 2016

   D. 2021

9. Messi scored a spectacular freekick in the 2018/19 Champions League semifinal against_____?

    A. Liverpool

    B. Juventus

    C. Bayern Munich

    D. PSG

10. How many goals has Messi scored at the FIFA World Cup?

    A. 11

    B. 12

    C. 13

    D. 14

10 Trivia Answers

1. C – Ronaldinho

2. B – 2007

3. D – Estonia

4. A – Osasuna

5. B – Arsenal

6. C – Xavi

7. B – 2

8. D – 2021

9. A – Liverpool

10. C – 13

PUZZLE SOLUTIONS

M J M E E P W J C Y Z R O X Z N Z L A T
O T Z O P W R M T Y E L F Y E V M B N Q
I X M F Q A R W N Q L A G I L L L P I Y
V N U W H N O C R D K P X T A M T L T Y
W Q O G J C S Y O S B U G G G K N T N T
J G Z Y G U A B D K J L B G C C N E E R
V J O U X I R O N T O G C U B G W S G W
E A Q F T M I R O C P A E X H V V D R P
O B O L B Z O Y L W A R G K E Z E Z A O
D M I K Y C W Y L Y I R L F S N L G Z X
T M G Z Y S L R A W F D P N O N B A N D
P A K Z T L X N B S D Q C I J N L T D P
K J R S L S A L B R N S L Z G O K L G E
I P S A A H L V Z N W C J H G J L Z A D
D M K U N K P P J H Y E N M S F V F F E
L O E D E Y V T F E J R J E G Z F H H W
J X A S P C P U C D I R O W R Z M R L B
D W L N S C D H N L A F P B F K G R Y U
X O G E K D X Z V I D I X D L E I E A M
D H B Z O L U H B G I S P W A B S T X U

1. LAOOTFLB   FOOTBALL
2. EPLAYNT   PENALTY
3. KCFRKIEE   FREEKICK
4. OOAZGL   GOLAZO
5. ELBIRBRD   DRIBBLER
6. YKRMAAPEL   PLAYMAKER
7. DTTFOEFELO   LEFTFOOTED
8. NOAELRABC   BARCELONA
9. PIRSA   PARIS
10. ROFRDAW   FORWARD

Messi

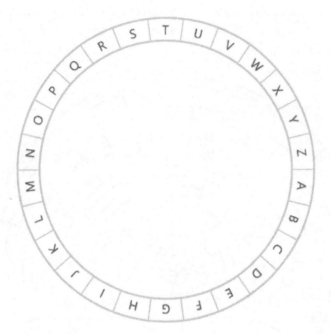

1. KZKHFZ   La Liga
2. JCM   Leo
3. EMJYXM   Golazo
4. ORF   PSG
5. YXOZBILKX   Barcelona

6. TBK   UCL
7. ODMZKSX   Penalty
8. BZLOMNT   Camp Nou
9. SCDY   UEFA
10. JBPPF   Messi

A. Penalty
D. La Liga
G. Leo
J. Barcelona

B. UEFA
E. Messi
H. Golazo

C. PSG
F. Camp Nou
I. UCL

Solution

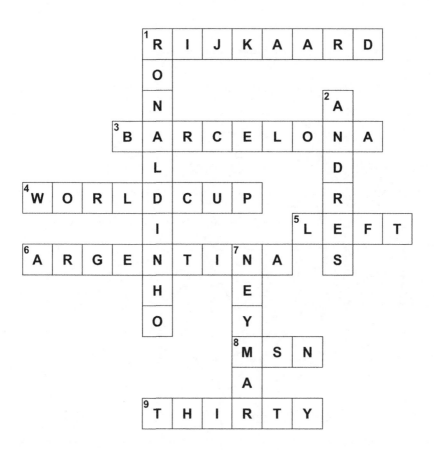

Across

[1] Messi's first coach at Barcelona
[3] Messi's first club
[4] Messi's biggest trophy
[5] Messi's strong foot
[6] Messi's nationality
[8] Messi's trio in 2015
[9] Messi's number in PSG

Down

[1] Assisted Messi's first goal
[2] Messi's middle name
[7] Messi's Brazilian friend

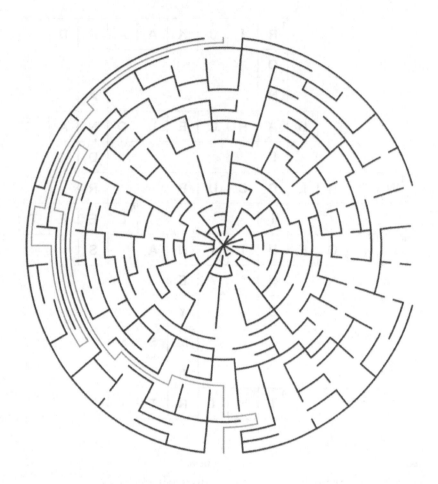

J	J	Z	P	J	B	U	H	Q	I	F	R	K	H	Q	Q	A	V
G	H	C	H	N	N	P	D	O	X	H	F	A	W	L	B	M	J
S	C	F	F	P	H	F	Q	D	R	E	L	P	F	V	Q	F	Q
W	C	V	L	Z	F	N	W	Z	K	I	I	F	I	U	G	Y	X
Q	A	R	U	B	W	S	K	Y	Y	C	H	C	K	J	Q	V	F
J	N	G	D	Z	S	T	R	I	K	E	R	B	S	I	U	I	U
L	V	Q	J	H	X	A	E	N	O	L	L	A	Y	B	A	Z	B
B	G	K	O	X	A	Y	S	D	K	D	K	S	R	U	R	H	Y
L	G	N	E	G	R	A	R	O	Q	M	D	M	Y	V	M	I	M
W	D	I	N	O	F	B	S	H	E	L	U	J	C	B	S	F	Q
P	D	J	T	I	N	W	Z	Q	U	L	K	P	D	Y	Q	B	N
Q	F	N	Z	L	A	B	D	M	S	Y	A	U	A	M	D	O	K
B	I	R	K	I	O	G	H	G	J	Z	P	W	N	O	C	V	M
B	O	D	L	E	N	J	O	J	H	T	W	O	S	E	N	D	K
L	L	W	F	P	I	I	W	F	S	S	C	I	I	A	A	P	V
E	D	Q	Q	L	M	B	R	G	J	A	R	E	M	Q	O	C	
R	W	O	R	L	D	C	U	P	P	L	A	Y	M	A	K	E	R

Solution

			¹C									
			H									
		²R	A									
		I	M									
		G	P	³M			⁴S					
		H	I	I			U		⁵C			
		T	O	D			A		O			
		W	N	F			R		P			
⁶P	A	R	I	S	S	A	I	N	T	G	E	R	M	A	I	N
I		N		E			Z		D			
Q		G		L					E			
U				D			⁷L	A	L	I	G	A
E					⁸P				R			
				⁹B	U	S	Q	U	E	T	S	
					Y				Y			
					O							
					L							

Across

[6] Messi's French club
[7] Spanish national league
[9] Barcelona Spanish #5

Down

[1] European Cup
[2] Messi's first position
[3] Messi's current position
[4] Barcelona Uruguayan striker
[5] Spanish national cup
[6] Barcelona Spanish #3
[8] Short Spanish center back

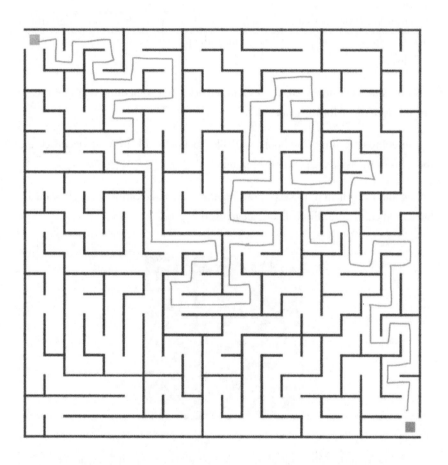

With love, from The House of Ballers team…

Hello our fellow FootBaller.

We really hope you enjoyed *MESSI: The Complete Story of a Football Superstar.*

From the bottom of our hearts, thank you for purchasing and reading it to the end.

We create these books to allow people to, not just expand their knowledge around their favorite clubs and players, but to keep the passion we all have for the game lit and alive.

Life can come with many challenges and setbacks. But something that never leaves our side is our love for the game.

If you enjoyed reading this book, we'd like to kindly ask for your feedback and thoughts in the review section on Amazon.

This would really help us to keep spreading the word and creating the highest quality books and content for football fans all across the globe.

>> Scan the QR Code above to leave a short review on Amazon <<

Thanks in advance!

Ball out,

The House of Ballers team.

Made in United States
North Haven, CT
13 November 2023

43944613R00065